COURT YARD HOMES

Joann Plockova

COURTYARD HOMES

THE MODERN COURTYARD HOME

JOANN PLOCKOVA

Our desire to connect with nature is elemental. Exposure to sunlight, fresh air, and green views has been proved to reduce stress, calm minds, and clear lungs, among other benefits. Biophilic design—design based on principles that enhance that connection—has not become a top priority just because it looks and feels good, but because as we are further and further immersed in the digital world, our bodies, minds, and hearts crave the natural world even more. When the pandemic came along, that craving grew stronger. And along with it came a desire for private natural space in our own homes where we could feel connected while still protected and comfortable.

Offering just that, the courtyard home is a tradition that dates back centuries. In China, for example, there was the *siheyuan*—a series of buildings surrounding one or more courtyards. In ancient Rome, the atrium impluvium home, with a water catchment system in its central courtyard. Adapted to their specific location and surroundings, these internal spaces around which the homes and lives of their inhabitants revolved were a means of fresh air, a source of connection with one another, and a way to bring the outside in. Today, there are new breeds of courtyard homes, many informed by or extending vernacular forms, that are doing the same and so much more. Welcome to the modern courtyard home. This book offers a look at some of the most innovative, inviting, and inspiring examples from around the world.

In Akashi, Japan, House in Akashi (page 42) appears from the outside like a carved wooden box. Once inside, the compact home reveals its courtyards, all three of them. Together, the softly lit trio, planted with trees, surrounds the main living space and creates for the family of four who live there a feeling of being immersed in the forest. Casa VO (page 120), in Puerto Escondido on Mexico's Pacific Coast, not only incorporates a courtyard, but it *is* a courtyard. Its architect, France-born, Mexico-based Ludwig Godefroy, reduces this residence—one in a set of four identically designed duplex holiday homes—to its essence through a simple material palette of concrete, wood, and brick. There is little to no division between outside and inside; the two merge into one. In Sydney, Australia, TRIAS transformed a formerly damp and dark terrace house for a couple and their two pets into the Hidden Garden House (page 128), a peaceful, pared-back home with green views all around thanks to the addition of a vitrine-like courtyard. Situated on the ground floor, it is also visible from the home's green roof above. Inspired by the homeowners' love for Japanese design and architecture, the courtyard brings in light, air, and a feeling of calm contemplation.

The courtyards in all of these homes admit light. Often the homes take the shape of their long narrow plots and need a means to bring daylight into their far-reaching spaces. Or they are set in temperate climates characterized by their cloud cover, such as the Courtyard House (page 110) by Leckie Studio in Vancouver, or Cork House (page 178) by Polysmiths in London (the home of Polysmiths's founding architect Charles Wu). But these courtyards also serve as a means of passive cooling in hot climates such as San Antonio, Texas, where Susan's House (page 148) by Mary English and Xavier Vendrell Architects is located; Mexico, where Práctica Arquitectura's Casa Ederlezi (page 50) is found; or the Mediterranean, where courtyard homes have a long tradition because of the region's high temperatures.

No matter their locations, many of the homes in this book incorporate the courtyard as an organizing element. Often set at the center of the home, the courtyards create zones among the spaces that surround them. They simultaneously demarcate and unite different areas. Functioning as additional rooms, they merge with the interior and extend the livable space. The interior rooms become part of the courtyard, the courtyard becomes part of the rooms. The courtyards often can be closed off or opened with the simple sliding of a door. Parents can keep an eye on their kids. Couples can stay connected. All inhabitants gain unique perspectives.

There is an element of surprise with a courtyard. From the outside, many of the homes are private and closed. But once inside, the homes open up. There is a feeling of release, as architect Gurjit Singh Matharoo says of Cut, Fold, Bend, Play (page 158), a monolithic, multicourtyard home his eponymous firm designed in Chennai, India. There is also a feeling of sanctuary—an escape from the hustle and bustle of the city in urban environments, and in others, busy professional lives and all of life's stresses. Inside, these internal-facing homes feel contemplative and joyful. They are private but offer a constant relationship to nature. Sky, earth, and plants merge with the interior. Inside becomes outside.

Often framed in glass, these landscaped spaces—adorned with native grasses and flora in some homes; artfully arranged with potted plants or a single tree in others—provide sight lines to green. The idea of a continuous landscape is also achieved. As with Can Jaime i n'Isabelle (page 190) in Majorca, Spain, a barely-there home designed by TEd'A Arquitectes, architecture becomes one with both the surroundings and the interior landscape. Developing into its own microclimate, which helps to cool the house, the central courtyard was designed with many plants that will overtake it over time. Nature takes precedence over architecture. "The architecture will slowly recede," as architect Toby Breakspear of Australia-based Breakspear Architects says. The courtyard becomes its own living, breathing thing.

A calming focal point, the home's defining attribute, its source of identity, its center, the courtyard *is* the house. Like material palettes, these courtyards of various shapes and sizes add texture and depth. They transform homes and define them, offering entirely new internal landscapes.

For homeowners, courtyards contribute to a rich daily living experience. They offer a sense of tranquility and contribute to wellness. "There is now a sense of peace and calm when they arrive home and spend time there," says TRIAS cofounding director Jennifer McMaster of the inhabitants of Hidden Garden House, who notes that the green additions "contribute significantly to their mental health and well-being." By connecting those who live inside to the benefits of nature through these courtyard homes, the hope—as Breathe architects say of the homeowners of Edgars Creek House (page 30) outside Melbourne—is that they will live happier, healthier lives.

GREEN UNIVERSE

COURTYARD HOUSE FOR TWO BOYS

VINHEDO, BRAZIL

SHIEH ARQUITETOS ASSOCIADOS

Pages 16–17: “Paulista architecture”—a strain of brutalist architecture that developed in Brazil in the 1950s—“embraces a preference for [the] rational organization of space and geometry, alongside the utilization of exposed raw materials,” says architect Leonardo Shieh of the home’s architectural influences. “This aesthetic not only highlights the beauty of simplicity but also celebrates the tolerance of imperfections and the passage of time, adding depth and character to the architectural design.”

Previous: The austere palette of exposed concrete blocks, with concrete beams and panels, was chosen with the idea that it will improve with the passage of time. The finishes follow the same thinking: flooring is either hardwood or Portuguese mosaic stones.

Opposite: The courtyard is grounded by a single yellow flowering ipê tree, whose delicate blooms last for only about two weeks a year. "There is, therefore, a year-long anticipation for this event," says Shieh.

Below: The courtyard is the home's organizing element. Each of the four pavilions, including an outdoor living area with a barbecue, was designed to have a constant connection to the courtyard.

Just three- and five-years-old when they moved in, the sons of São Paulo-based architect Leonardo Shieh have enjoyed the first years of their childhood playing in their own private courtyard. In the morning, they and their parents can step onto the grass, just feet from their beds, and cross to the kitchen for breakfast or to the indoor lap pool for a dip. "With two young sons, our aspiration was to create a central space where life could unfold effortlessly," says Shieh. "Fostering a strong sense of family connection."

Grounded by a single yellow ipê tree (native to Brazil and highly symbolic in Brazilian culture, Shieh says), the square-shaped courtyard became the predominately single-story home's locus. Including a mezzanine and greenery that hangs over the sides of the planted roof, the four-thousand-square-foot house is made up of a quartet of interconnected, largely glass pavilions arranged around the courtyard. "We envisioned every room oriented towards the same open, grassy area, maximizing opportunities for shared experiences and togetherness," says Shieh.

Opposite the courtyard from the single-story bedroom pavilion is an outdoor living area with a barbecue. Above it, a terrace that extends out from the mezzanine reads like a footbridge. Adjacent to the bedrooms is a double-height living room/dining room/kitchen pavilion. A wooden louver on its upper facade provides shade for the rooms behind it and adds a distinctive texture. Across the courtyard from this main living pavilion, and bounding the courtyard on its fourth side, is the enclosed, single-story indoor lap pool pavilion. "A strategy to burn off our boys' energy," Shieh says. The back wall is adorned with white ceramic tile panels with a dynamic geometric pattern in dark green.

Shieh, his wife (a psychologist), and the two boys moved in just before the pandemic. The architect carved out a studio for himself and continues to spend most of his time working from home. As planned, the lush central courtyard space has become the family's green universe. "It brings nature remarkably close to each room," Shieh says enthusiastically. "From our beds, we enjoy sightings of small lizards in the morning and small marsupials in the evening."

Pages 22–23: Adding to the lush greenery of the surroundings are a variety of monstera and philodendron, and the occasional unexpected addition. "Sometimes, by a stroke of luck, we find cherry tomatoes or melons growing, likely from seeds brought by birds, right by our living room," says Shieh.

Previous: The patterned ceramic tiles on the back wall of the swimming pool pavilion were designed and custom-made by Brazilian artist João Nitsche, a family friend.

Opposite: Light, vegetation, and sky become elements of the architecture. By stepping right outside their bedrooms, the architect's sons can immerse themselves in greenery.

Above: Heated by solar energy, the lap pool is "a meditative place," says Shieh, "like a ryokan's onsen."

Overleaf: Hardwood floors soften the concrete material palette, along with a wood sunshade that adorns the double-height living/dining/kitchen space with dappled light. The artwork above the fireplace is by Erica Mizutani.

HOUSE AS LANDSCAPE

EDGARS CREEK HOUSE

COBURG, AUSTRALIA

BREATHE ARCHITECTURE

Pages 30–31: Timber battening is a defining feature of the home.

Previous: The home's three adjoined pavilions frame the central courtyard and look out to the landscape, including Edgars Creek, after which the house is named.

Left and below: The house and courtyard are designed to recede into the landscape, prioritizing shelter and sanctuary.

Opposite: Careful attention has been paid to filtering the hot summer sun with punched openings and timber screens and shades throughout the pavilions.

On its west-facing side, this house in a suburb of Melbourne opens up to a landscape that includes ironbark trees, sandstone cliffs, and the creek after which it is named. Driven by the clients' desire to create a physical and spiritual connection to its surroundings, the house was designed to extend right into the landscape and to invite it inside. "Our clients wanted to experience the warm air in summer and the crisp air in winter," say the architects, Melbourne-based Breathe Architecture. "They wanted to be connected to nature and its seasons, as opposed to being in a hermetically sealed, artificial environment."

The home is made up of three adjoined pavilions, each clad in ironbark except for a wall of rammed earth on the southmost, street-facing side. One pavilion is for living, one is for bathing, and one is for sleeping. They are connected on the west side by a breezeway. Informed by the path of the sun, the views, and the breezes off the creek, the home's "open-air spine," with its timber brise-soleils, simultaneously ventilates the house and shades it, "producing a micro environment while filtering light through its screen," the architects note. Inside, the passageway is lined on both sides with plantings, including a lush gathering of indigenous plants tucked under a floating staircase to the second floor and a native *Xanthorrhoea australis*—or grass tree—growing from a cutout in the walkway. Reinforcing the relationship to nature established on the exterior, the U formed by the pavilions and breezeway frames a central courtyard. "Edgars Creek House

is all about a connection to nature," says Breathe. "This home is about the landscape in which it exists, and the courtyard offers a way to live as part of that system rather than trying to preside over it."

With a ground cover of mulch and leaves from the surrounding trees, this courtyard is planted with a scheme centered around the Australian ecosystem and inspired by the ironbark trees of the surrounding site. "We wanted to provide an environment where native insects and animals could flourish," the architects note. "We looked to local species for planting to restore the native plant habitat and preserve this biodiversity."

The surrounding interior spaces open to the courtyard with little separation. One corner of the living room, lined with a window seat in wood, fully opens to the landscape, allowing the owners to sit among the trees while still inside. "The intent behind the courtyard was to provide additional amenities, more landscape outlooks, more light," the Breathe team says, "and for the residents to move between the interior and exterior spaces with ease, connecting them to the benefits of nature in the hope that they would live happier, healthier lives."

Below: A ground-floor bedroom looks out to the landscape.

Opposite: The courtyard was carefully crafted with materials that seamlessly blend with the natural surroundings, creating an inviting extension of the home's living space.

Previous: The brise-soleils filter natural light and promote ventilation year-round. There is no glass between the battens, although the enclosed ceiling provides protection from the rain.

Below: From the breezeway, a set of floating stairs leads to the second floor, where there are two bedrooms, a playroom/den, and a deck.

Opposite: The rammed-earth facade is a twin wall construction with an insulated core, maintaining the building's stable indoor temperature year-round.

44

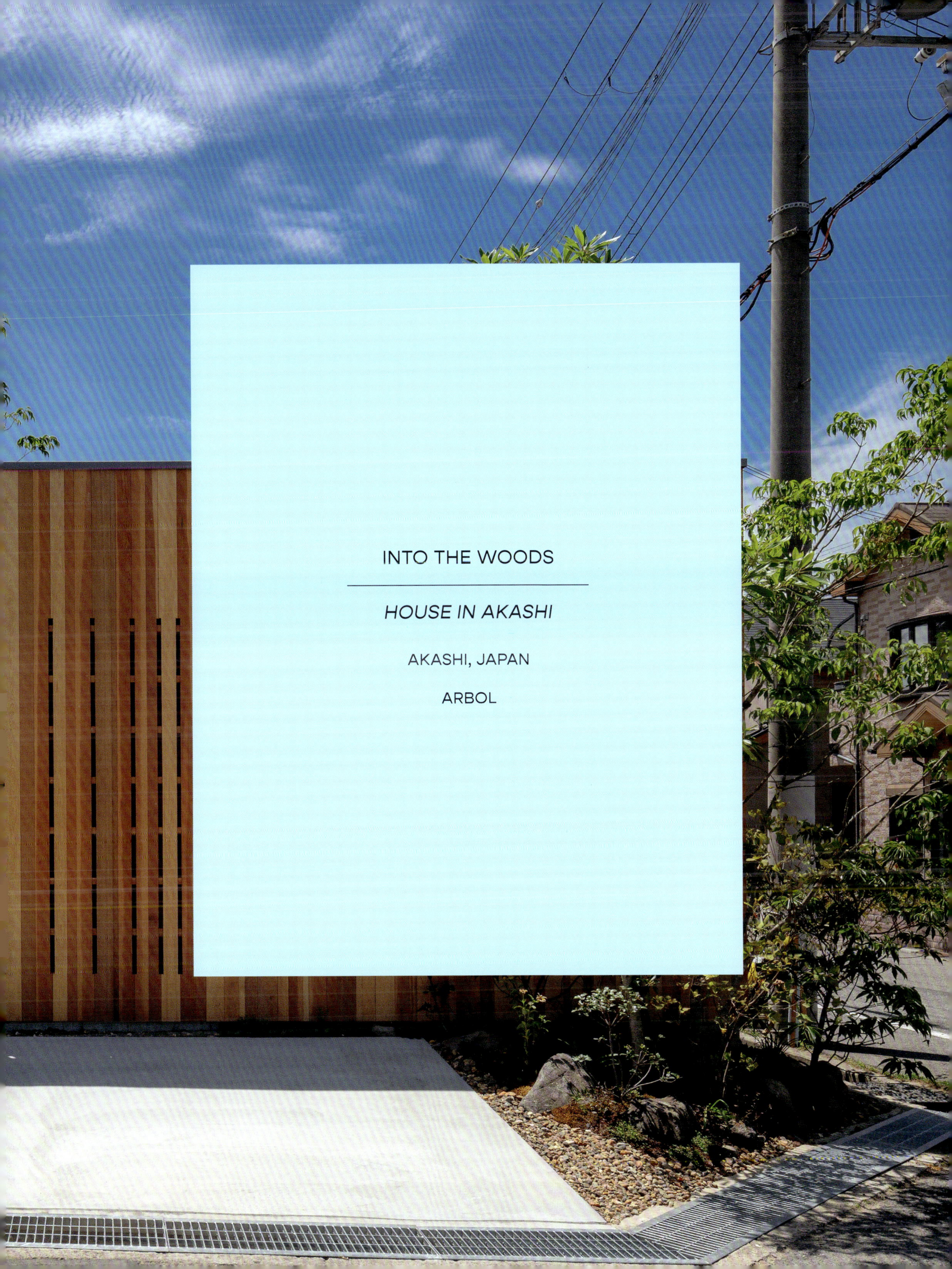

INTO THE WOODS

HOUSE IN AKASHI

AKASHI, JAPAN

ARBOL

Previous: The compact, cedar-clad home's closed external nature contrasts with the openness of its interior.

Below: A view of one of the three courtyards from the side of the house where the bedrooms and other private spaces are located.

Opposite: Cedar, Japanese cypress, spruce, and other wood types were used not only for the house's exterior, floors, and furniture, but also for furring strips, joists, and rafters.

From the outside, this home in Akashi, a coastal city in Japan's Hyōgo Prefecture, reads like an exquisite jewelry box carved from wood. The subtle detailing of its facade—punctuated by vertical slits to promote ventilation and admit light—allows for privacy within and in the evening seems to emit a warm glow. Open it up, and the home's interior reads almost like an inversion of its exterior: closed becomes completely open, wood becomes a woodland.

The compact, single-story home was designed by Arbol for a couple and their three children. In pursuit of a rich daily living experience for the family, the architects incorporated three courtyards "harmonizing with the wind, the sunlight, and lifestyle," the architects say. In a calming blend of cedar, spruce, Japanese fir, and other wood varieties, the home's interior is divided into three sections, each with its own courtyard. Overall, the residence creates a feeling of being immersed in a forest.

The first of the home's three courtyards is found at the entrance, where a wood-burning stove offers a warm gathering place for the family come winter. With wood-framed glass doors on three sides, this courtyard has a graveled floor and a tree that rises beyond its pergola ceiling. On its far side, opposite the entrance and the stove, the courtyard is connected to a traditional tatami room where a low, ground-level window offers a unique perspective into the second courtyard, "a yard with a kitchen garden," as the architects describe it. The family enjoys harvesting the fruits of a grapevine planted there.

These two glass courtyards wrap around the main living space, the open-plan living room/dining room/kitchen, as does the third courtyard, this one located just across from the entrance. Connected to the bedroom area and the kitchen, sight lines into this "yard for viewing" are directed through both a low-lying window, like the one in the tatami room, and an upper-level window. "It is designed to enjoy the extraordinary scenery, not only at noon, but at night," the architects note. "The yard's plantings will become visible by turning off the inside lights and using the outside lights."

Just like its contrasting exterior and interior, the home's personality shifts by day and by night. Each time of day, like the seasons, provides a different connection with the outdoors while inside. "It brings new little discoveries into daily life," say the architects.

Previous: The tatami room offers views into all three courtyards from various perspectives.

Opposite and above: Daylight streams into the house like "waves of sunshine through the trees," the architects note.

BREATHING FROM THE INSIDE

CASA EDERLEZI

SAN PEDRO GARZA GARCÍA, MEXICO

PRÁCTICA ARQUITECTURA

San Pedro

OPTIC

Pages 50–51: From its roof terrace, the house connects its owners to panoramic views of the Cerro de las Mitras mountain range.

Previous: The home is built on a narrow plot in the historic center of San Pedro Garza García in Monterrey.

Left: "The geometry of Ederlezi draws inspiration from Balkan ziggurats," says architect David Martínez, "a concept influenced by the clients' travels and specifically incorporated as a formal and conceptual element of the project."

Opposite: The courtyard divides the home into two volumes.

"Whenever someone new visits the house, they are very pleasantly surprised to discover something they did not imagine from the outside," says architect and Práctica Arquitectura founder David Martínez of Casa Ederlezi, this dusty pink- and rustic red-toned home he designed for good friends in the historic center of San Pedro Garza García in Mexico's Monterrey. The house—the zigzagging stepped form of its facade reminiscent of the mountain ridges in the distance, its influences ranging from northwestern Mexican residences (with their high, flat roofs and facades punctured by few openings) to Mozarabic architecture—sits on a narrow sixteen-foot-by-twenty-foot plot. Despite the lot's humble size, the goal was to create a home that feels expansive, that "breathes from the inside," Martínez says. "We have always been interested in the idea of going outside in."

The architects took the project as an opportunity to challenge the typical typology of the area's homes—fully enclosed houses on long, narrow plots where, once inside, the only connection to the exterior is through windows. For their friends, they wished to create a more dynamic living experience that varies throughout the day, and from day to day, with the sunlight and weather. The house's interior comprises a series of surprising pathways pushed along the outside edges, which allows for more habitable space in the center. This circuit of interstitial, meandering halls acts as an organizing element around the home's defining feature, the courtyard. "In the end, the courtyard is the

project," says Martínez. "It is what makes the house make sense and order."

Immediately upon entering, the home takes you back outside. A zaguan, or passageway, leads into the central courtyard. On one side, above the entry, is a double-height guest room with a roof terrace. On the far side are a sunken living room and the kitchen, and above them, the primary bedroom with its own landscaped terrace overlooking the courtyard.

The sculptural courtyard is bounded by simple wood-block benches and lined underfoot with *tezontle*, a terra-cotta-colored volcanic rock. The homeowner—a landscape architect, designer, and passionate nature lover—planted xeric plants and a *duraznillo*, or wild peach tree, to provide shade. The courtyard is a great captor of light for the house, Martínez says. During the day there is no need to use artificial lighting. There is also little need for air-conditioning as open windows in combination with the courtyard create a cross breeze. "It is only necessary to turn on the air-conditioning maybe twice a year," Martínez says. "The rest of the time the house is resolved by passive systems."

Living with a private, cool, interior green space is the owners' balm from the busy, hot city. "The integration of vegetation as an organ of the project and not as a dressing [is important]," says Martínez. "Here everything lives together as a single organism."

Page 56–57: The arrival through a passageway into the courtyard makes for a pleasant and human welcome, Martínez says, one that offers a calm transition from the busy city outside.

Previous: Ederlezi is the name of the celebration that marks the beginning of spring in the Balkans and Turkey. The contrast between the greenery of the vegetation with the red tones of the walls, the *tezontle* in the garden and the doors, emulates memories of desert and Mediterranean landscapes present in conversations with the clients during the design process.

Below and opposite top: The main living spaces on the ground floor of the house's rear volume connect to the courtyard through floor-to-ceiling glass and their shared color palette.

Right: The primary bedroom on the upper floor of the rear volume features its own terrace garden topped by a roof formed from branches of ocotillo, a plant indigenous to the Southwest United States and northern Mexico.

Overleaf: "Ederlezi house reconciles notions such as the fluidity of an ethereal and open space with the privacy that allows a separation of daily life from the streets," Martínez says.

LANDSCAPE FOR LIVING

COURTED HOUSE

SYDNEY, AUSTRALIA

BREAKSPEAR ARCHITECTS

The borders between landscape and living space are blurred in this home for a young family not far from Sydney's center. Here not only does the house revolve around its central courtyard; so too does the life of the occupants.

The homeowners, two busy professionals with children, requested a retreat and, fundamentally, a garden as an additional room of the house. This suggested to the architects an internal escape where neither architecture, nor interior, nor landscape takes precedence, but rather are joined together in a rich, interconnected "ecology of life," where the house frames the sky and the rhythm of daily life moves with the sun and the vegetation at its center.

In a regional take on the traditional walled courtyard house, the architects inverted the classic Australian wraparound veranda typology and adapted it for the urban setting. "A central courtyard provides a city version of 'bush,' around which the home privately revolves," says architect Toby Breakspear. "The whole interior opens to become a veranda to this bush; garden and home made inextricably one."

The house is essentially a series of rooms oriented around the central courtyard. The four bedrooms make up the outermost layer. These quiet spaces, each occupying their own corner, include mezzanines overlooking the rooms. The gallerylike, double-height shared spaces, including the entryway, kitchen, dining room, and living room, are adjoined to the courtyard physically and materially by the home's defining cedar-clad beams.

Pages 64–65: Sixteen-foot ceilings and deep cedar-clad beams unify interior and exterior.

Previous: Glass blocks to the northeast and frosted windows to the southwest bring soft light to the interior while focusing views inward.

Below: The home's shared spaces are double-height rooms that are defined by deep cedar-clad beams.

Opposite: "Complexity comes not from the architecture," says architect Toby Breakspear, "but from the reciprocal relationships that emerge when the experience of dwelling is attuned to the surrounds."

"Corridors are not required, ensuring an ease of movement between spaces and the constant presence of nature in every direction," says Breakspear.

Surrounded by operable aluminum-framed glass doors on all sides, the central courtyard tucks a cluster of tropical plants, under a myrtle canopy, into a retained garden rectangle at one end of what is otherwise deck. Moments of nature unify the front yard, interior courtyard, and rear yard, creating a through line of green. "Courted House is a framework of clarity that will support a lifetime of coexistence between a family, their garden, and the surrounding city," says Breakspear. "It is a home where demanding professions are swapped for pottering with plants and playing with kids."

Previous: The home's rectangular plan is a grid of nine rooms oriented around a central courtyard.

Left: On the exterior, perforated steel screens and cement panels filter views of the surrounding streets and houses.

THROUGH VIEWS

BV HOUSE + OFFICE

BRUSSELS, BELGIUM

BRUNO VANBESIEN ARCHITECTS

Architect Bruno Vanbesien's home in Brussels benefits from its position along a park. When he and his son sit outside on the roof garden terrace, they don't just have great views, they appear to be immersed in them. From this vantage, father and son can also look down into two interior courtyards one floor below. These spaces bring air, sunlight, and kinetic sight lines into the ash and timber relief-concrete interior of what is not only Vanbesien's home, but also his office. "The inner courtyards add light and transparency to our house. One can see from the office through the courtyard into the kitchen and vice versa," Vanbesien says. "Although it is very difficult to catch in the pictures, because of the multiple reflections, in reality one can see through different barriers, the different reflections giving the space an ever-changing atmosphere."

The hybrid home/office is the renovation of a town house and a former bakery on the ground floor. Before Vanbesien got his hands on it, the ground-floor space was dark and enclosed. "The plot originally was fully [built out]," says Vanbesien. "And therefore, the ground level didn't get much natural light, nor views." Today it is where his office lives, along with the home's dining area and kitchen.

Previous: The reorganization of the town house, which had included a bakery on the ground floor, was designed to fully embrace the home's location along a park and to bring in more light.

Below and opposite: The smaller courtyard behind the kitchen was designed to admit light and views into the lower floor.

The smaller courtyard is tucked behind the kitchen. You can prepare food at the stove and look into the vitrine-like space and up to the sky. To the left, via a set of angled steps that lead to the dining area, you can walk into the courtyard. "We covered the floor with many pots of plants," Vanbesien says, "a bit like the courtyards in Spain." From here you can see into the office and further, like an enfilade, into the second, larger courtyard, and its delicate tree. "We only planted one tree, the *Gymnocladus dioicus*, the Kentucky coffee tree," says Vanbesien. "This tree was selected because of its very small, transparent leaves."

Surrounded by the L-shaped office on two sides, this larger courtyard is open to the park beyond through windows cut into the exterior wall on one side. In the warmer months, branches of the park's trees spill in through the frames and plants grow between the floor tiles, giving the courtyard the appearance of a ruin reclaimed by nature.

Back inside, on the private upper levels, accessed through the kitchen and up a set of steel floating stairs, the backside of the otherwise copper-clad home is almost fully glazed, reinforcing the home's constant connection to the landscape.

Page 78: The courtyards create visual connections between home and office.

Previous: Bricks from the former ground-floor bakery were incorporated into the existing garden wall. Windowless frames allow plants and tree branches from the adjacent park to spill inside the larger of the two courtyards.

Opposite: The glazed rear facade of the copper-clad home extends the interior living space outside.

IN THE CLOUDS

MUSUBI HOUSE

PA'AUILO, HI, USA

CRAIG STEELY ARCHITECTURE

On any given day the weather here along the northeast slope of Mauna Kea on the Big Island of Hawai'i can quickly transform from clear blue skies to driving rain and high winds. It was a challenging spot to build a second place to live and work for two creative directors from California, but they were enamored with the panoramic views of ocean and inactive volcano, and by the surrounding windswept grasslands of their one hundred acres, which move likes waves on the sea when the winds pick up.

Designed to embrace those conditions, their home, cast in concrete, with floor-to-ceiling glass exterior walls, takes the shape of a triangular volume below a diamond-shaped roof. "Like a ship's prow, the sharpest end of this triangular house deflects the formidable wind," says the architect, Craig Steely. The home, which is completely off the grid thanks to photovoltaic panels and a rainwater collection system, is built around a five-hundred-square-foot interior courtyard at its center. "The huge atrium allows for protected outdoor living in all weather conditions," says Steely. With a floor lined in slabs of pahoehoe (a local basalt lava rock), the courtyard demarcates in the interior the house's three zones—the bedroom/bathroom, the living room/study, and the kitchen—while curved concrete walls at the end of each point of the larger surrounding triangle delineate the exterior. "Spaces flow from zone to zone while always remaining in visual contact with the rolling landscape," Steely says. On two of the courtyard's walls, sliding pocket doors open to create a seamless interior-exterior connection.

In one corner of the courtyard, a native Hāpu'u fern grows, its fronds spilling into the kitchen and living room. On the atrium's north side, Raphis palms and local ferns act as a privacy screen for the primary bed and bath and the guest suite. "We consciously chose mostly endemic plants that can survive and thrive with little maintenance," Steely notes.

Previous: "The owners came to us with a simple request," says Steely, "Make a house that embraces the nature of the windswept grasslands of the Hāmākua Coast."

Left: Sliding doors on two sides of the courtyard retract into the walls, resulting in a seamless connection between the interior and the courtyard.

Overleaf: "The clients' willingness to prioritize permeability over privacy gave us the freedom to create a plan without doors or hard boundaries," says Steely.

When the weather changes, Musubi house (so named because it resembles the popular local snack Spam musubi, the Hawaiian version of Japanese *onigiri*, a similarity pointed out by a carpenter while reviewing the plans), allows the owners to remain outdoors even when indoors thanks to the size and orientation of the atrium. "When clouds roll through, the atrium creates a micro climate zone inside that allows the clouds to float into the house," says Steely. "You can pass through clouds to get from one zone of the house to another."

Left: A sunken seating area is positioned in one of three rounded corners that delineate the softly triangular building's interior.

Above: The guest bathroom is defined by its curved concrete wall and circular skylight.

Overleaf: The site consists of valleys with seasonal creeks and expansive fields of wainaku grass. "The wind blows up through the long valleys and fields, making the grass roll and swell," says Steely.

TREE OF LIFE

PEAR TREE HOUSE

LONDON, UK

EDGLEY DESIGN

Previous: Built around the home's pear tree, the central courtyard draws the house inward, "with windows facing onto this courtyard," says architect and homeowner Jake Edgley, "which keeps the house private from the many neighbors to either side."

Below: The dark and gold-accented vertical cladding speaks to the qualities of the surrounding trees.

Designing their own home is a chance for any architect to experiment. For architect Jake Edgley, an unusual plot in a backland site in South London's leafy Dulwich neighborhood presented that opportunity. The site was during the Victorian era a fruit orchard. Growing on it was a 140-year-old pear tree. Wishing to retain the tree, Edgley wrapped the home around it. For the past ten years, the poetic tree has been the center of life for the architect and his family.

From the start, Edgley sought to turn the house inward. He envisioned a home arranged as a linear series of rooms, each oriented toward an introspective main courtyard. In this courtyard, the tree is the centerpiece. "The courtyard forms the central focus point of life within the home," says Edgley, "and is the space in which the experience of moving through the house revolves."

Clad in a dark siding accented with thin, vertical gold articulations that speak to the surrounding trees, the house comprises a pair of two-story volumes. Those volumes—with private bedroom space on the upper floors and shared living space on the ground floors—are connected by the central courtyard and a glass walkway that traverses it. Glazed on three sides with one rear wall planted with ferns, the contemplative central space brings into the home light and long views. "The effect created is like having a huge terrarium in the middle of the house that can be seen and enjoyed as you walk around the house's different spaces," Edgley says.

On either side—the playroom on one, the main living space on the other—large sliding doors open up to extend the connection between inside and outside and to encourage airflow. The glass panels of the walkway are articulated with large timber columns with gold accents that reflect the dappled light created from the tree. "All south facing glass is solar coated; however the tree provides natural shade," says Edgley.

At the time Edgley was designing his family home, he watched *A Single Man*, which was partly filmed in John Lautner's Schaffer House. "This inspired both the midcentury aesthetic of warm timber tones," he says, "and views of rooms through planted courtyards with non-perpendicular walls to create diverging reflections in the glass." The sculptural form of the home's pear tree, with its gracefully outstretched limbs, is visible in those reflections and throughout the house, including from the bedrooms upstairs. The tree's constant presence is a source of calm and connection, solidity and strength. After all, it's the foundation upon which Edgley's family home was built. "I was the architect, client, and contractor on this project, which allowed us to evolve the design and experiment with ideas as the house was built," he says. "This allowed us to create a building that has a close relationship between interior and exterior."

Previous: Slate flooring runs continuously from the courtyard to the bridge walkway, giving the impression that the bridge is a roof floating above an open space, and blurring the boundary between the interior spaces and the courtyard.

Opposite: Upper-level bedrooms are also afforded views of the sculptural tree.

Below: Glazing enables views through the house and across the courtyard, "which adds to the sense of depth and complexity of the house," Edgley says.

OPEN BOOK

LIBRARY HOUSE

BOLLNÄS, SWEDEN

STUDIO FRIA FOLKET

Located on the edge of a sparse pine forest with views of Lake Voxsjön on its south-facing side, this house in Sweden's historic Hälsingland province has its own rhythm. You can imagine the owners, a ceramicist and lawyer, quietly padding around the warm red-tiled floors of the cozy pinewood-and-glass home throughout the day.

The residence's plan is in part inspired by the vernacular architecture of the area, in which farmhouses are arranged around a central cobblestone court, but has been updated to meet the specific needs of the homeowners, who desired spaces for their passions where they could create and work both alone or together. "The design of the house needed to strike a balance between privacy and connectivity," says architect Hanna Michelson of Studio Fria Folket, "allowing each occupant to work independently while still enjoying each other's company and presence." The house's four adjoined volumes—one for cooking and gardening; one for arts and crafts; one for law, science, and music; and one for sleeping—are organized around the courtyard according to the sun's movements and the personal rhythms of the couple; the sequence begins with the kitchen and greenhouse garden and ends with the sleeping quarters.

The home was also designed to accommodate the couple's extensive book collection. Looping around the interior edges of the approximately two-thousand-square-foot house is a gallery of bookshelves. Visible through floor-to-ceiling glass sliders, the library

Pages 100–101: In order to reduce the environmental footprint of the house, the walls and roofs have been constructed plastic-free and insulated with flax fibers according to vernacular traditions of the area.

Previous: The gabled volumes are mainly closed on their exterior facades, with the exception of the south-facing volumes, which open up to the surroundings, including Lake Voxsjön.

Above: The kitchen is linked to a greenhouse.

Left: In line with Nordic building traditions, one of the studios has been constructed so that it can be isolated from the rest of the house when the temperature drops.

Opposite: "Moving through the different parts of the house like a thread, the book gallery binds the volumes together in accordance with the adjoining section," says architect Hanna Michelson.

frames the central courtyard. Together, the book gallery and courtyard blur the lines between inside and outside, and where the library begins and ends. The courtyard becomes an "open-air reading space," says Michelson, "a room defined by its purpose rather than its physical limitations."

The courtyard—its patterned brick floor sunken within a timber border and punctured by two squares accommodating an Aronia bush and small tree—was inspired by the tradition of monastery courtyards, "which influenced a design that facilitated a mindful circular movement, internally as well as externally, around the courtyard," says Michelson.

No matter where they are in the house, whether they're together or in their own worlds, the home allows the couple to be connected to one another and the rhythms of their surroundings.

Page 106: The design of the courtyard was in part inspired by the ancient Roman compluvium: an underground tank collects rainwater that falls into the courtyard (which is then used to water plants in the greenhouse).

Previous: In pursuit of further sustainability, the house was customized to the family's existing furniture.

Right: Organizing the home around the courtyard enables visual contact between the separate volumes.

PRIVATE TRANSPARENCY

COURTYARD HOUSE

VANCOUVER, BC, CANADA

LECKIE STUDIO

Pages 110–11: From the rear porch, you can look through the kitchen and courtyard, all the way to the front of the home.

Previous. Despite the house's relatively small proportions, it feels expansive.

Left: From the inside, the front yard and neighboring houses are visible, while wooden louvers obscure the interior from the street.

Above: A soothing color palette of grays, green, and pale wood contributes to the home's serene feel.

Standing on the street, it's possible to see straight through to this home's rear garden. While the architects created privacy through a slatted wooden screen facade, much of the home—designed in the canon of West Coast modern homes—is completely transparent, its windows looking onto gardens inside and out. "The project embodies biophilic design principles to create an intimate connection with a carefully constructed garden, which occurs as three discrete natural spaces," says architect Michael Leckie, founder of Leckie Studio.

Those three natural spaces include the front garden, the rear garden, and, between them, the middle "third yard": an interior courtyard. "[The courtyard was designed] to expand the psychological experience of connection to nature in all the spaces," says Leckie. Open to the outdoors at its rear, west-facing side, where a trellis with climbing plants creates a privacy wall, the courtyard is entirely glazed on its other three, interior sides. Bordered by the living room, the kitchen, and the dining room, the courtyard includes a stone path and a terrarium-like landscape that (intended to be somewhat wild) varies throughout the seasons with plants that flower at different times of year. "We

have incorporated full height glazing at three sides of the main floor to allow as much light into the house as possible, and as much connection to the courtyard," Leckie says. "The north and south glazing walls are operable, so that the courtyard flows freely into the interior spaces."

Juxtaposing privacy and transparency, the house was designed for a couple and their child. "The owners love the house so much. They constantly say to me, 'Sometimes I can't believe I get to live here,'" Leckie says. While the street level features floor-to-ceiling windows and sliding doors, upstairs, where the roofline slopes toward the courtyard, creating dramatic vaulted ceilings, more discreet windows open onto the courtyard from the office and the primary bedroom, "creating a dialogue between the two levels," Leckie notes. The entire home, including the upper walls of the courtyard, is clad in western red cedar. This materiality, together with the modestly proportioned home's signature courtyard, creates a feeling of expansiveness and serenity. "The courtyard expands the perception of all the spaces on the main floor," says Leckie, "and creates a private oasis in the city."

Previous: The kitchen, with the courtyard on one side and the rear yard on the other, is grounded by a monolithic stone island.

Opposite: "We always search for the one big idea or specific opportunity that is unique to each client/project," says architect Michael Leckie. "In this case, the relatively small program and modest budget encouraged us to propose that the clients build a small house. The smaller footprint allowed us to insert the courtyard into the middle of the building."

OPEN TO THE ELEMENTS

CASA VO

PUERTO ESCONDIDO, MEXICO

LUDWIG GODEFROY

In Puerto Escondido, a small town on the Pacific coast of Mexico known for its surfing, winter doesn't exist. With this as a starting place, architect Ludwig Godefroy wished to truly blur the lines between interior and exterior in this residence, one in a series of four duplex holiday homes, where you never know if you are inside or outside. "It's another way of living, people have to accept it," Godefroy says. "Sometimes you can have bats inside. It's part of it."

Godefroy flipped the classic courtyard-home scheme on its head, starting with the interior garden and building the sculptural, cave-like concrete house around it: This is not a home with an interior courtyard, but an interior courtyard as a home. "The house *is* a courtyard," he says. The only components suggesting enclosure are two massive wooden doors at the entrance. But, having entered, there are no windows, no glass, just voids—massive twin circular openings cut into the sloping concrete roof planes. One frames the home's interior garden. From it, a planted palm tree emerges. Alongside, birds-of-paradise, a banana plant, monsteras, succulents, and cacti are able to endure the tropical region's strong sun. Just opposite, the second oculus frames a swimming pool, which extends into the home under the shelter of sloped concrete. "The swimming is inside and outside of the house at the same time," Godefroy notes.

Previous: In Puerto Escondido, a small beach town on Mexico's Pacific coast, there is warm weather all year long. "Protection against the cold is not needed," says architect Ludwig Godefroy. "The houses only have to provide shelter against the sun and rain."

Right: Godefroy describes the matching vacation homes as a simple expression of a house as a cave—"a house where the wind is always blowing through." The only doors are at the entrance.

Brick is the primary accent to the dominant, monolithic concrete. Extending from the brick plane of the courtyard area, three brick steps lead into the sunken lower level, and the kitchen. There, behind a curved concrete partition are a bedroom and bathroom. Also from the courtyard area, a set of cantilevered concrete stairs leads up to the mezzanine and a second bedroom and bathroom, the shower hidden behind a rounded concrete element. Light pours through an open skylight.

Informed by his upbringing in Normandy, with its historic, World War II–era concrete bunkers, and by the pre-Hispanic temples and pyramids of his adopted home, Mexico, Godefroy distills architecture to its essence. He strips away the unnecessary to achieve simplicity. "My vision of architecture focuses on changing people's habits rather than looking for technological improvements, toward a simpler way of living with fewer necessities, to minimize our impact on the ecology of our planet," he says. "It's my idea of what's sustainable, a vernacular sustainability."

Page 124 and previous: "The project blurs the border between in and out to become a singular habitable garden," says Godefroy, "where everything remains open all day and all night."

Right and opposite: The sculptural nature of Casa VO is visible in the staircases—the steps to the kitchen and those leading to the upper floor—and the curve of a concrete enclosure concealing a bedroom and bathroom.

21

GREEN VIEWS

HIDDEN GARDEN HOUSE

SYDNEY, AUSTRALIA

TRIAS

As homeowners Laura and Aman move through their transformed terrace house in Sydney's Darlinghurst neighborhood, they enjoy glimpses of verdant foliage. On the ground floor, an L-shaped extension wraps around an interior courtyard in which a Japanese maple reaches upward toward the light. Above, the extension is topped by a green roof with grasses planted in deep soil and trailing plants that hang down into the courtyard, toward the maple. "It's now possible to see greenery from every room in the house," says TRIAS cofounding director Jennifer McMaster.

The couple—she is a ceramicist, he a digital experience designer—called on local studio TRIAS to transform the formerly dark, damp, and cramped terrace home into an oasis of calm within the dense, inner city outside their door. Drawn to Japanese design and architecture, Laura and Aman (who share the home with their cat, Erik, and dog, Annie) wanted their residence to embody the quality, craft, and tranquility they embrace as an approach to life. Both the pared-back home and its unexpected green interventions were inspired by traditional Japanese temples and the sense of peace found within them.

Visible upon entry, the courtyard brings natural light and fresh air into the surrounding kitchen and dining room nook, and beyond. Framed in Victorian ash, sliding and pivoting doors create an exterior-interior connection and allow the owners to enter the garden where sandstone—recovered from underneath the house during excavation—is incorporated as stepping stones, pebbles (which help with drainage), and a large sculptural boulder reminiscent of what might be found in a traditional Japanese rock garden.

Along with the terra-cotta tiles forming the kitchen floor, Laura handmade the white tiles that line the upper walls of the courtyard on three sides. In addition to connecting the indoors and outdoors visually, these glazed tiles reflect the light and diffuse it toward the ground floor and are a satisfyingly tactile contrast to the smooth, white-painted bagged brick walls and rigorous millwork of the kitchen.

Upstairs, the roof garden is visible from a window in the stairwell and most notably from the shower, where pivoting windows frame the green view. Together with the courtyard, this upper garden has transformed how the home is experienced and brought Laura and Aman a profound sense of well-being. "Amid the hardness of the inner city, these gardens bring something soft, gentle, changeable, and life-affirming," says McMaster. "And seeing these gardens constantly grow and evolve is a beautiful and precious thing."

Previous: The original pink facade of this Sydney terrace house offers a warm welcome to the home's interior transformation.

Above: In the upstairs bathroom, the shower offers views to the green roof.

Opposite: The courtyard is the heart of the house, providing a nature-filled outlook for the downstairs rooms and peaceful, private green space to look onto upstairs.

Page 132: Windows and doors slide or pivot, bringing the outside in and extending the home into the diminutive garden.

Previous: "When we first met, we were all drawn to Dieter Rams's aphorism 'less but better' and resolved to create a home that would embody this ideal," says architect Jennifer McMaster. The design, which decreased the interior floor space, took courage from our clients. What they gained was a vastly improved home, which is bright, welcoming, and breathable; true proof that less can be more."

Opposite: "The garden is always growing and changing, which gives life and interest to the home," says McMaster. "It is a piece of unexpected delight revealed in an otherwise commonplace Sydney terrace."

GREEN DREAM

SKYGARDEN HOUSE

NHA TRANG, VIETNAM

PHAM HUU SON ARCHITECTS

Pages 136–37: SkyGarden, in Nha Trang, Vietnam, brings nature in as the rapid development of urban environments across the country impacts green space.

Previous: Greenery, which spills out from voids in the facade, offers shade, privacy, and an immersive experience to those inside.

Below: The house's highest space is dedicated to the family altar, "providing privacy and solemnity," says architect Pham Huu Son.

Opposite: Three generations share the home. On the top floor, the primary bedroom for the young couple extends into the courtyard.

Vietnam's favorable climate conditions, including seasonal winds, abundant sunshine, ample rainfall, and high humidity, are highly conducive to the growth of dense plant life. Yet as the country's urban areas continue to develop rapidly, green spaces are gradually disappearing. For architects, this, in combination with limited lot sizes, presents a challenge. "Consequently, small-sized homes are forced to fulfill multiple functions, resulting in cramped town houses devoid of greenery," says architect Pham Huu Son.

SkyGarden, a multigenerational home in Nha Trang, a city on the southern coast, is a striking example of Huu Son's firm's approach to "returning natural greenery to the living environment" in hopes of encouraging others to do the same. "Our focus lies in designing styles with abundant natural greenery interspersed within living spaces," says Huu Son, "fostering a stronger connection between people and nature while reducing air pollution and dust within homes, and providing comfort and relaxation."

The towering three-story home is a kind of green dreamscape. Its front facade gives the impression of opening like a book to reveal its signature courtyard. Foliage spills out from the voids of various shapes and sizes that punctuate the walls; it resembles a kind of gallery of green, each window a frame.

Throughout the interior, leafy flora is tucked into terrarium-like vitrines and built-in planters, offering shade and privacy. But the home's highlight is its elevated courtyard garden on the third floor. "We were aiming to evoke the feeling of being in an outdoor garden," says Huu Son. Including a carpet of green grass and a lush landscape of kaffir lime trees, ferns, dracaena, and devil's vine, this interior greenscape was designed as an extension of the primary bedroom. The garden grows across three tiers, with wooden steps and stone pathways gradually ascending to the highest level, which looks out to the surrounding landscape and the verdant mountainside in the distance. A concrete bench at the base of the parklike courtyard's centerpiece, a star fruit tree, is a place of quiet contemplation.

The courtyard is separated from the interior by a succession of glass panels. "There is no sense of division between the garden and the indoor spaces," says Huu Son. "They blend almost harmoniously together." To prevent heat build-up, gaps between the panels allow hot air to escape and cool air to enter. A glass-covered pergola-like roof that extends from the interior to the courtyard also incorporates openings, allowing for airflow and "night dew and rainwater to pass through, nurturing the plants below," says Huu Son.

From there, a set of stairs leads up to the fourth floor, where the family altar is located. "Worshipping is a part of Asian culture. Thus the highest space of the house is dedicated to the altar, providing privacy and solemnity," says Huu Son.

The house—an oasis within the dense urban fabric of Nha Trang, has been transformative for its inhabitants. "The family has a serene, elevated garden that has sparked a new hobby of practicing yoga before starting their workday. Harvesting sweet fruits from the tree in the garden also brings them unexpected joy," says Huu Son "Every morning, the sounds of birds singing, along with the sight of them building nests and laying eggs, creates a vibrant living space."

Pages 142–43: A concrete bench beside the star fruit tree provides a contemplative spot to take in the view from the uppermost part of the courtyard.

Previous: The home's green facade folds into the landscape, echoing the verdant mountains in the distance.

Below: The ground-floor pool adds an additional layer of visual interest and passive cooling.

Opposite: The lowest level of the ascending courtyard connects with the indoor spaces, then gradually rises to reduce the soil load.

THREE IN ONE

SUSAN'S HOUSE

SAN ANTONIO, TX, USA

MARY ENGLISH AND XAVIER VENDRELL ARCHITECTS

429

433

From the street, Susan's House resembles any modest single-family home. But upon closer inspection, the varying orientations of its rooflines are a subtle hint to something different inside.

The 1,900-square-foot home was built for architect Mary English's sister Susan. Susan wished to move to San Antonio's historic Lavaca neighborhood so she and her family could easily bike to the city's River Walk, museums, and parks. While they appreciated the neighborhood's close proximity to downtown, they assumed that a trade-off would be a private backyard like the one they enjoyed at their former home in the suburbs.

A desire to maintain private exterior space in an urban context was part of the inspiration behind the home's surprising and delightful incorporation of not one, but three interior courtyards. This unusual move—one that came naturally to co-architect Xavier Vendrell, who, originally from Barcelona, "was born, raised, and educated in the tradition of courtyards," English says—was also a response to the conditions of the site. "The lots in this section of the historic Lavaca

Pages 148–49: A bird's-eye view of the 1,900-square-foot house for architect Mary English's sister and her family reveals the home's unique form.

Pages 150–51: The house's neighborhood, Lavaca, is one of the oldest in San Antonio and is on the National Register of Historic Places.

Previous: The courtyards are similar in size, form, and materials to the other rooms of the house.

Below: A picture window in the living room looks out to the first of the three courtyards, an outdoor foyer with storage for bikes.

Opposite: A view of the first courtyard, just inside the front door.

neighborhood are narrow and deep," English says. "And the traditional typology of the neighborhood results in little opportunity for a relationship between interior and exterior."

English and Vendrell took advantage of the lot's depth by stretching the home across it and creating space for the three courtyards as well as a front porch—a requirement of the neighborhood's historic design guidelines. Through the solid wooden front door, the home opens to the first of its three courtyards, designed as an outdoor foyer with storage space for bikes. From here, a second wooden door leads into the residence's interior, revealing the home's long lines and open plan. "This second door accesses the interior of the house with courtyards, crossed and diagonal views, and transparencies," says English.

Surrounded by the open kitchen, dining room, and living room (bedrooms are tucked out of sight), and framed by large sliding glass doors, the two central interior courtyards were designed as rooms of the house. "The perimeter walls are white stucco so they can read as a continuation of the interior white walls. The gray gravel on the courtyard floor reads as a continuation of the concrete floors on the interior," English says. "All the material choices were based on the courtyards as rooms of the house."

Besides defining the spatial character of the home, the courtyards also contribute to maintaining the comfort of the interior by passively cooling the home. Their southeast orientation brings in plenty of natural light in the mornings, while during a good portion of the afternoon the courtyards remain in shadow due to their orientation, narrow dimensions, and the paloverde tree planted in each. Additionally, "at night the temperature of the roof cools and the cooled air moves down the slope into the courtyards," English says. "The large sliding doors and ceiling fans draw the cool air into the heart of the house."

For Susan and her family, their new urban setting allowed them to maintain three special outdoor spaces, right inside their home.

Right: This room between two interior courtyards was designed as a screened porch. "Courtyards are a good solution for the climate in San Antonio," says English. "[They] serve as collectors of cool air."

OPEN FROM THE INSIDE

CUT, FOLD, BEND, PLAY

CHENNAI, INDIA

MATHAROO ASSOCIATES

Suspended from above, stairs, slabs, and beams become abstract surfaces that appear as movable planes in this Jenga-like house in raw concrete. Almost completely column-free (a signature of the architects), the ground floor feels expansive. "We had to open the house from inside to offer views," says architect Gurjit Singh Matharoo, founder of Matharoo Associates.

Located within the dense urban fabric of Chennai, in southern India, the home was designed for a couple, their three daughters, and regular visitors, including a large extended family and others: "Being socially religious, the family accommodates many sages who come and stay here," says Matharoo. The site's small parcel is tightly bound by buildings on three sides; the challenge for the architects was to maintain privacy while also bringing in light, air, and views.

Borrowing from the model of the traditional Indian courtyard home, in which rooms surround and open onto a courtyard, this house, which appears impenetrable from the outside, is punctuated by a series of interior courtyards that admit the elements and reinforce the impression of continuous space. "A concrete plane envelops the periphery to form a monolithic

Previous: The house is located on a small cul-de-sac in Chennai, India, with three neighboring buildings surrounding it.

Above: Upon entry, the staircase frames the view of the central courtyard.

Opposite: Large voids are carved out from within, bringing in ample light, air, and greenery.

Below: “The planes cut, bend, and fold to create a perceptible notion of movement within the house,” says architect Gurjit Singh Matharoo.

Opposite: The architects describe the home as a cocoon that cuts off the chaos of the city.

shell that shields its contents from the world outside," says Matharoo. "It is only upon entering that the plane unfolds to reveal its hollowed center."

Immediately on entry, the house offers a direct sight line to the central courtyard. Framed by the zigzagging lines of the staircase and other suspended architectural elements, the indoor-outdoor space—with a carpet of grass, tall trees that extend above the roofline, and plants that add texture and contribute to indoor air purification—brings daylight and green views to different parts of the house through various cutouts. It also both segregates and connects the surrounding common areas and more private spaces.

Upstairs, where the bedrooms are located along with a large lounge that looks down to the ground floor, other, smaller courtyards are placed around the axis of the main courtyard, creating further visual connection and encouraging breezes. "Although the building looks very solid and closed from the outside, actually all rooms are cross ventilated," Matharoo says. Skylights and windows onto the courtyards are thoughtfully placed to ensure privacy while admitting additional light, which casts an ever-changing display of shadows along the concrete walls throughout the day. Instead of looking out, this house looks within, and architecture, interiors, and landscape become one. "The courtyard enhances the quality of life," says Matharoo, "by fostering a close connection to nature within the family's urban dwelling."

Left: "Leaving materials in their natural form creates a connection with the context and exposes the original deep-rooted quality the materials hold within," says Matharoo of the raw concrete.

Overleaf: "When you go to a building, it must elevate you," says Matharoo. "There is a heightened feeling that we have that keeps pulling us back again and again to the same place."

MY OWN PRIVATE GREENSCAPE

COURTYARD RESIDENCE

SEATTLE, WA, USA

MWWORKS

From their upper-level bedroom, the owners of this house on a sloped site in Seattle can walk out onto their planted roof terrace and feel like they are alone in their own private garden above the city. Their expansive view includes Lake Washington, the Cascade mountains, and the city of Bellevue in the distance. Two interior courtyards offer an inward-focused alternative to the omnipresent views and are spaces in which they can relax in nature more privately. "These negative spaces create a foreground of intimacy with light, earth, air, and native plantings," says architect Steve Mongillo, cofounder and principle of mwworks, "in contrast to the expansive framed vistas of water, mountains, and sky that are ever present in the distance beyond."

For this family of four—a couple and their two teenage children—the house, which is so strongly connected to its surroundings, has provided a sense of calm and a greater appreciation for light and nature. "The house has made me a better person," said one of the owners, admiringly, just months into living there.

Pages 168–69: The courtyards are bathed in natural light and lush with native vegetation.

Previous: Built on a double corner lot in Seattle, the house was scaled to fit in among neighboring houses and designed to preserve several significant trees, including a redwood, and large pines to the north and west.

Below: A glass breezeway connects the front and rear courtyards.

Opposite: "In Seattle, sunlight can be elusive and often diffuse," says architect Steve Mongillo. "So it is a welcome pleasure to have the garden courts washed in natural light."

Overleaf: With the curtains open, the dining room is emersed in the courtyard.

Pages 176–77: An upper-level bedroom overlooks the rear courtyard.

The two courtyards merge into one long line of landscaping. Selected for scale, year-round interest, variety of texture and color, and interaction with light and wind, the key plantings for the courtyards are sculptural Pacific Fire vine maple trees, grounded with grasses, ferns, and perennials including Japanese sweet fire, black mondo, Corsican hellebore, and Lenten rose; and creeping lily turf and wild ginger as ground cover, along with large stones that stand out among the green.

The first courtyard, at the entrance, offers a through line to the second courtyard, which frames the open living room and dining room. They are adjoined in the middle by a full height, glazed breezeway. Together, they offer a segue between the public and the private, and a poetic pause between the home's active areas.

Comprising a single-story pavilion to the west and a double story pavilion to the east, the highly textured home constructed of earthen concrete, cedar, and other renewable natural materials, was designed to balance privacy with connection. "Open and modern but still deeply connected to the landscape," says Mongillo, "this single-family house is designed to be a calm respite from the hustle and bustle of Seattle."

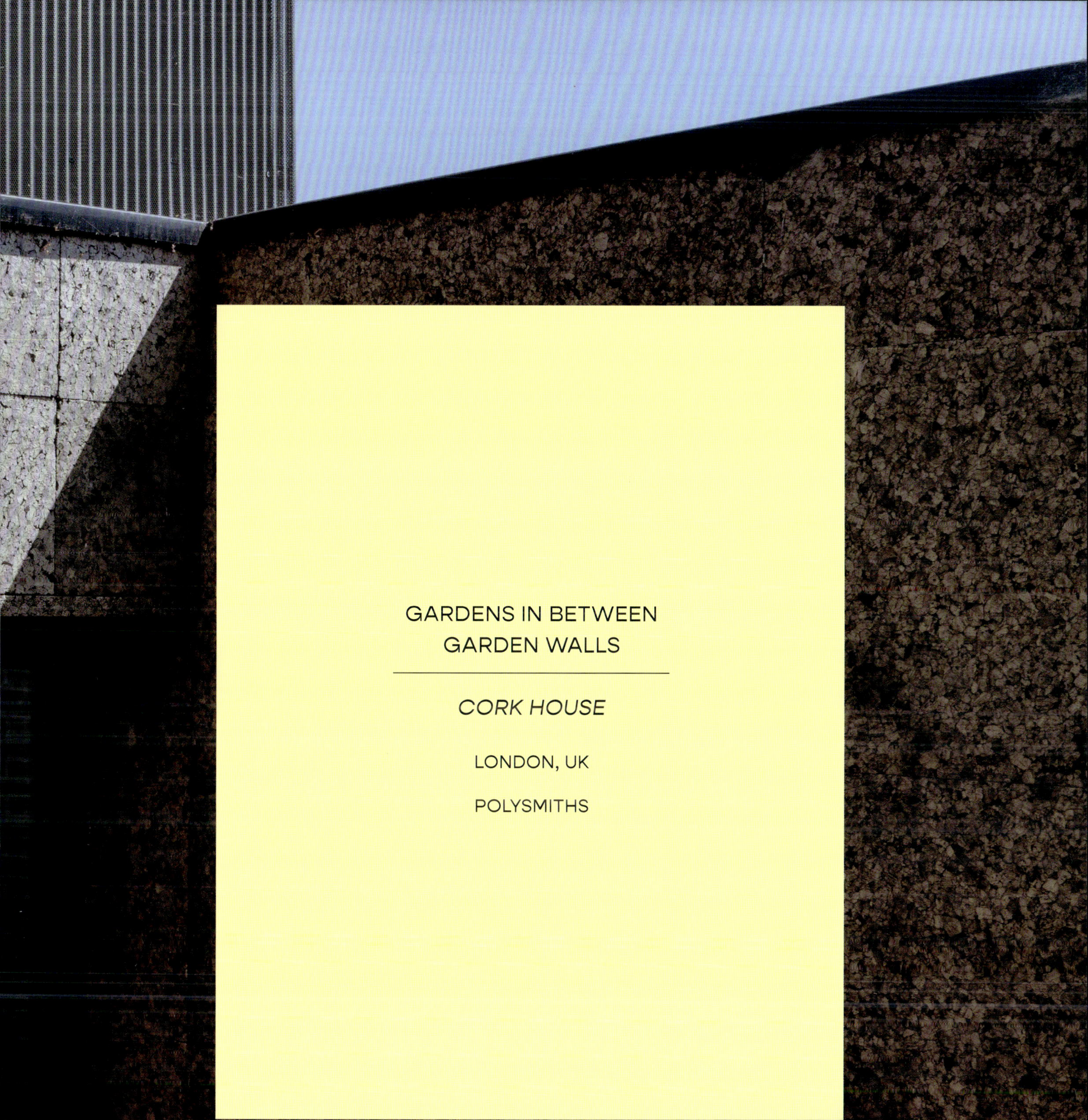

GARDENS IN BETWEEN GARDEN WALLS

CORK HOUSE

LONDON, UK

POLYSMITHS

Even on the quietest summer days, there is always a breeze passing through architect Charles Wu's calm, cork-paneled, three-bedroom home in East London. In 2020, Wu bought the narrow plot on a backland site that sits in between the walled gardens of the neighboring terrace houses. The constraints of the site presented a challenge: how to promote light and ventilation in a lot surrounded by a brick boundary wall.

Inspired by small town house courtyards of homes in Tokyo, "as well as more traditional Kyoto *machiya* courtyards," Wu adds, the architect punctuated the 1,500-square-foot home with two courtyards and a light well. "Living in London, where private outdoor space is at a premium, having courtyards is a gentle luxury that brings light and plants into the home," says Wu. "[A courtyard] is a quiet oasis that softens the building and creates interest all year round."

Creating a distinct identity for the courtyards was important. "We wanted each courtyard to feel different, from a *tsubo-niwa*-type courtyard with a simple planting scheme in the living room, to a

Pages 178–79: Architect and homeowner Charles Wu purchased the plot in East London in 2020 and set about producing plans for a three-bedroom family home. "We used cork as a means to sidestep the construction supply chain issues during the pandemic," says Wu of the material lining much of the house.

Page 180: When the folding doors are opened, the courtyard merges with the open living/dining/kitchen, creating one large space. "It is good for summer parties," says Wu.

Previous: A pathway leads to the front door of the house, which is hidden from the street.

Above: The kitchen benefits from additional light through a tall, vertical window looking into a second courtyard.

Left: A lightwell—the third courtyard—brings daylight into the primary bathroom and a cross breeze into the adjoined primary bedroom.

Below and overleaf: Light streams into the living room from the main courtyard.

'breakfast room' courtyard facing the master bedroom," Wu explains. But most important was to create spaces that are visually and physically connected to the rooms around them, "and find ways to connect them into a whole," says Wu.

To compensate for London's gray days and admit as much sunlight as possible into the spaces, Wu oriented the courtyards and most of the windows toward the south. The main courtyard sits in a southerly corner of the open-plan space containing the living room, dining room, and kitchen. Framed by the pink-tinted brick boundary wall, which Wu hopes the climbing rose he introduced will one day blanket, a grouping of potted smoke bush, berberis, magnolia, and pampas grass sits artfully atop the graveled ground, which is flush with the interior floors. When the courtyard's folding glass doors are fully open, the inviting space becomes part of the room. "We used concertina glazing that slides away, with no corner posts and frames hidden away into the walls," Wu says. "In this way the indoor and outdoor spaces become truly connected."

Opposite: The south-facing bedrooms look out to the second courtyard.

Below: The primary bedroom, located on the ground-floor level, opens onto the "breakfast room," the second courtyard.

Overleaf: Courtyards are contained spaces that are easy to maintain, says Wu. They are also spaces where plants can thrive, as they are sheltered from harsh wind and direct sun.

The second, centrally located courtyard—situated just behind the kitchen and running from the ground floor all the way up to the top floor—separates the shared living spaces from the bedrooms by offering privacy and muffling sound. It brings precious light into the kitchen, through a tall, slender window, and into the bedrooms that surround it. On a lower split-level, the primary bedroom opens up to the courtyard through concertina glazing. A light well, located in the furthest corner of the home, allows sunlight into the bathroom there and on the upper floor, which includes two additional bedrooms.

The courtyards and the residence are further unified through the use of cork cladding, inside and out, which gives the home a pleasant woody smell and contributes to its cozy atmosphere. Open and airy, warm and bright, Wu's home is full of light and ambience.

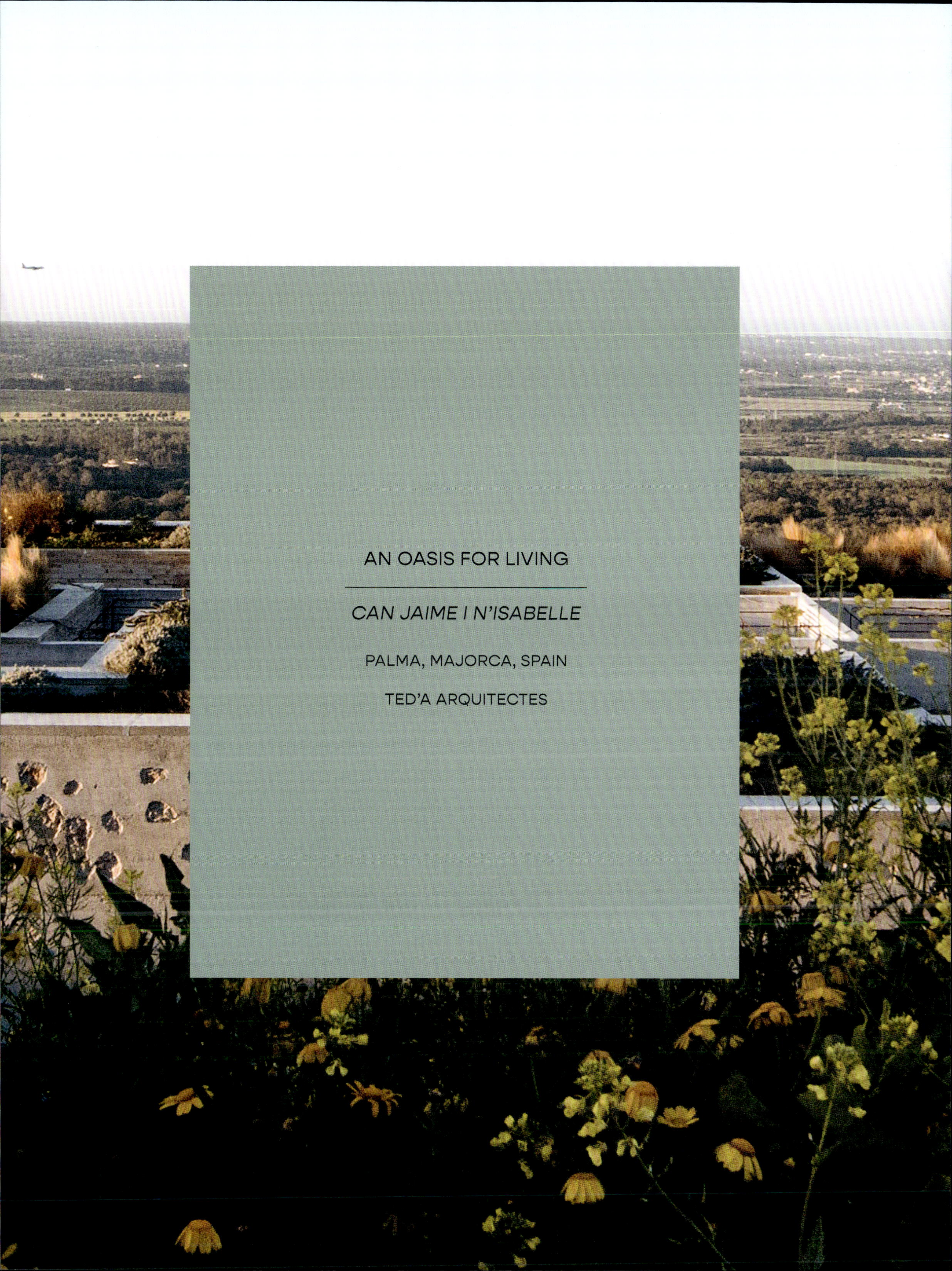

AN OASIS FOR LIVING

CAN JAIME I N'ISABELLE

PALMA, MAJORCA, SPAIN

TED'A ARQUITECTES

Time is a principal material in this house on the island of Majorca that was designed not only to disappear into its landscape, but also to become the landscape—it has grown into its surroundings, and its surroundings have grown into it. "The house is living," says Jaime, the homeowner, along with his wife, Isabelle, who completes the sentence: "The house is living with us."

Built for the couple and their two daughters, the namesake home is embedded into a steep south-facing incline. Blanketed by a green roof planted with native shrubs and grasses, the barely-there home carries on the Mediterranean architectural tradition of the patio, or courtyard, house. "A simple geometry and a compact volume are the results of a home that attempts to pass unnoticed," says architect Jaume Mayol, one half of TEd'A Arquitectes, along with cofounder Irene Pérez. From the outside, the home's walls of cyclopean concrete embedded with stones excavated from the surrounding grounds are fortress-like. But inside, walls made from Majorcan brick open to the central courtyard. "The patio is unexpected," says Mayol. "When you walk around the house you don't expect that interior space in that massive building. It's a nice surprise when you discover it."

An outdoor room, a place to come together, the courtyard is the home's central organizing element, around which the rooms are built. The courtyard was designed to be its own microclimate, acting as a passive cooling device for the home. Since its completion, the inviting space has also become an oasis of greenery and calm.

Pages 190–91: Built into a steep incline overlooking Bahia de Palma, the house is largely embedded into the earth.

Previous: The residence is organized around a courtyard, "heir to the Roman impluviums, brother of the possessions cloisters,"—a vernacular Majorcan form—"or the nineteenth-century patios in the center of Palma," says architect Jaume Mayol.

Above and opposite: Vegetation in the courtyard decreases the temperature of the space. "In summer, the patio becomes the main room of the house," says Mayol.

In contrast to the house's nearly monolithic peripheral walls, the shady space offers a visual and sensory experience incorporating ledges, edges, and voids in the concrete; verdant alcoves; and, everywhere, wood-framed windows in squares and rectangles at various levels and heights looking out and in, in and out. Creeping vines have taken over the walls and hang from the pergola ceiling. There are lush gardens in two corners; in another, a graveled garden where the couple grows herbs. Just opposite is a small pool with a fountain, the sound of the water carrying through the space. Elsewhere, a set of stairs leads up to yet more green space.

"The house belongs to this place," says Mayol in a video made for the international Brick Awards, for which Can Jaime i n'Isabelle was a Special Prize Winner. "The patina of time, the wrinkles, the rain, the green that grows, all these aspects are very important in order to understand the perfection of the imperfection, this natural way of becoming old."

Page 196 and previous: The plan of the house is approximately square and its rooms are arranged around the central courtyard, which features "porches" in each corner.

Opposite: While the exterior of the house is massive and impenetrable, the courtyard is human-scale and rich with openings at eye level.

Above and left: The materiality and spatial diversity of the courtyard carries into the interior.

Overleaf: The house has become a part of the hillside.

SKY GAZING

IGLOO

MOSSEL BAY, SOUTH AFRICA

YVZA

For their first house together after marrying in 2019, architect Yvette van Zyl and her husband, Dëon, a chemical engineer, wanted a laid-back home with a warm, lived-in feel, that would take advantage of its breathtaking site. "It has spectacular views toward the harbor and bay as well as the Outeniqua Mountains beyond that," says Van Zyl of the home the couple now shares with their eight-month-old son. Located in South Africa's historic Mossel Bay, where the climate makes outdoor living possible year-round, and inspired by the work of the late South African architect Gawie Fagan, the ship-shaped home features porthole windows, plenty of curves, and splashes of bold color that balance its rectilinear form and midcentury character.

To best take in the stunning view, Van Zyl designed the cantilevering home to face "20 degrees east of north" toward the bay and included in between the primary bedroom and the main living space a courtyard that increases the living space of the home and further connects it to earth, sky, and air. Including the whitewashed breeze-block wall and the adjoined back wall with its open window frame, the courtyard

Previous: The plot, overlooking Mossel Bay, "has no street frontage, which means total privacy," says architect Yvette van Zyl. "And it had enough space for an olive grove to be planted."

Below: Prioritizing "honest materials," including brick, marble, and wood, the house's design influences are "midcentury modern blended with some Japanese minimalism and craft," says Van Zyl.

Opposite: Brick pavers run throughout the interior, from the living and dining rooms to the courtyard, "so it all connects seamlessly," says Van Zyl.

Catherine &
John Pawson

can be enclosed on three sides, which helps to block prevailing southwesterly winds. When open, a sliding, stacking door extends the open-plan dining room and living area into the courtyard and the courtyard into the home. On the rear wall, a window from the courtyard lets light flood into a breakfast area just off the kitchen.

When guests are arriving, Van Zyl and her husband can see their friends climbing the stairs through the courtyard's westerly brick screen wall while they prepare food at the home's redbrick barbecue, a defining element of the residence's structure that runs from ground to sky, its chimney rising above the roofline. If the couple is not gazing at the sweeping view (or keeping an eye out for guests), they'll likely be looking up through the courtyard's large open oculus, which frames a snippet of the sky—with rushing clouds by day and the stars by night. "Summer nights are perfect for sleeping outdoors and stargazing," says Van Zyl. "The built-in bench is the perfect length for two adults to sleep on."

Although the family travels often, staying put can feel as refreshing, thanks in large part to the courtyard. "It connects the home directly to the weather and great climate. It makes the house bigger by practically acting as an extra room," says Van Zyl. "And it enhances the whole after-work sunset sundowner experience. It makes one feel like you are on permanent holiday."

Previous: The architecture is all about taking advantage of the hospitable climate and spectacular views.

Opposite: In the courtyard, the large "sky window," as the owner and architect calls the oculus, frames the sky and brings ever-changing light into the space.

FAMILY FOCAL POINT

CLIFTON HILL COURTYARD HOUSE

CLIFTON HILL, AUSTRALIA

STUDIO MKN +
ELIZA BLAIR ARCHITECTURE

Previous: Apart from a new picket fence, roof sheeting, veranda tiles, and a fresh coat of paint, the double-fronted facade of the original weatherboard worker's cottage remains the same.

Below: A window seat is a sunny spot to look into the courtyard.

Opposite: The courtyard includes a silver top ash timber deck, blond brick accents, and sleek black steel framing around windows and doors.

At the end of this home's long and narrow central hallway, the interior courtyard offers a breath of fresh air. Glazed on three sides with operable windows and doors that are framed in a crisp black steel, the insertion was designed to bring light into the depths of this south-facing home on a long, narrow plot.

The circa 1890s weatherboard worker's cottage was updated to accommodate a family of five, including twin toddlers and a teenager. Along with the addition of a flexible garden studio that could do everything from accommodate out-of-town guests, to serve as a teen cave, to act as a privacy wall, the owners requested a light-filled extension with an open-plan living area.

The interior courtyard, approximately 160-square-feet, is a focal point that visually connects the spaces that surround it. It is backed by a neighboring red-brick wall that warmly frames a deciduous tree that the family watches change colors through the seasons. On one side is a multipurpose room that can be used as an additional guest room. On another is the kitchen (windows into the courtyard allow parents to keep an eye on their toddlers while they prepare meals). On the far end is the living room, which offers views into and through the courtyard space. From the interior courtyard, you can look right out, beyond the open area of the living and dining rooms, to a bottlebrush tree in the backyard, which sits between the new, glass-and-brick extension and the black-clad garden studio addition adorned with metal mesh on which lush creepers will eventually grow. "The living room enjoys a dual aspect to two different landscaped spaces," says designer Meredith Nettleton of Studio MKN.

The home's interior, lined in ash, tile, and terrazzo, feels calm, cool, and cozy. Its blond brick— incorporated into window seats looking onto the courtyard and making up the rear facade—creates continuity between interior and exterior in harmony with its central courtyard. "The courtyard serves as a conduit for natural light and fresh air," says Nettleton, "effortlessly enhancing the flow of both throughout the entire floor plan."

LateNightTales

Previous: The courtyard effectively establishes a buffer zone, delineating the more private areas toward the front of the house from the expansive and communal living spaces located toward the rear.

Opposite: From the backyard, you can see right through the living room into the interior courtyard.

COURTYARD HOUSE FOR TWO BOYS, 2020
VINHEDO, BRAZIL
SHIEH ARQUITETOS ASSOCIADOS

4,000 square feet
Builder/Contractor: Reginaldo Carvalho
Engineers: WE Engenharia (Structural Engineer), Infraenge (MEP Engineering)
Interior Design: Shieh Arquitetos Associados
Landscape Design: Regen Ecossistemas
pp. 16–29

EDGARS CREEK HOUSE, 2019
COBURG, AUSTRALIA
BREATHE ARCHITECTURE

2,960 square feet
Builder/Contractor: Never Stop Group
Engineers: FORM Structures, Keith Long & Associates
ESD (Environmental Consultant): Nick Bishop ESD
pp. 30–41

HOUSE IN AKASHI, 2018
AKASHI, JAPAN
ARBOL (+ HASUIKE FOR DESIGN DETAIL)

871 square feet
Builder/Contractor: Sasahara Corporation
Landscape Design: Oginotoshiya landscape
pp. 42–49

CASA EDERLEZI, 2022
SAN PEDRO GARZA GARCÍA, MEXICO
PRÁCTICA ARQUITECTURA

1,722 square feet
Builder/Contractor: GC3
Engineer: Estructura mx
Interior Design: Práctica Arquitectura + client
Landscape Design: Oswaldo Zurita
pp. 50–63

COURTED HOUSE, 2018
SYDNEY, AUSTRALIA
BREAKSPEAR ARCHITECTS

2,150 square feet + storage lofts
Builder/Contractor: A.M. Custom Builders
Engineer: Cantilever
Landscape Design: Sprout
pp. 64–73

BV HOUSE + OFFICE, 2021
BRUSSELS, BELGIUM
BRUNO VANBESIEN ARCHITECTS

3,315 square feet
Engineer: UTIL
pp. 74–81

MUSUBI HOUSE, 2020
PA'AUILO, HI, USA
CRAIG STEELY ARCHITECTURE

4,400 square feet
Builder/Contractor: Kauhale Kilohana Builders
Engineer: Walter Vorfeld & Associates
pp. 82–91

PEAR TREE HOUSE, 2014
LONDON, UK
EDGLEY DESIGN

4,000 square feet
Builder/Contractor: Silverwood, New House Construction
Engineer: Hardman Structural Engineers
M&E Consultants: Mendick Waring
Landscape Design: Helen Robson Gardenia Gardens
Arborist: Wassells Aboricultural Services
pp. 92–99

LIBRARY HOUSE, 2022
BOLLNÄS, SWEDEN
STUDIO FRIA FOLKET

2,045 square feet
Builder/Contractor: Anders Jonsson
Engineer: Hanna Michelson in collaboration with BTKON and AFRY
pp. 100–109

COURTYARD HOUSE, 2021
VANCOUVER, BC, CANADA
LECKIE STUDIO

2,250 square feet
Builder/Contractor: Adisa Homes Ltd.
Engineers: Chalten Engineering, Terran Geotechnical Group
Interior Design: Leckie Studio
pp. 110–19

CASA VO, 2021
PUERTO ESCONDIDO, MEXICO
LUDWIG GODEFROY

1,600 square feet
Builder/Contractor: Obed Moreno
Engineer: Struk - Josué Hernandez
pp. 120–27

HIDDEN GARDEN HOUSE, 2021
SYDNEY, AUSTRALIA
TRIAS

500 square feet
Builder/Contractor: Zandt Building
Engineer: SDA Structures
Landscape Design: Studio Rewild
pp. 128–35

SKYGARDEN HOUSE, 2023
NHA TRANG, VIETNAM
PHAM HUU SON ARCHITECTS

4,305 square feet
Builder/Contractor: Nha Xanh 79 Company
Engineer: Nguyen Ngoc Thien
pp. 136–47

SUSAN'S HOUSE, 2024
SAN ANTONIO, TX, USA
MARY ENGLISH AND XAVIER VENDRELL ARCHITECTS

1,900 square feet
Builder/Contractor: Long House Builders
Engineer: GE Reaves Engineering
Interior Design: Mary English, Xavier Vendrell
Landscape Design: David Hill/Hillworks
pp. 148–57

CUT, FOLD, BEND, PLAY, 2018
CHENNAI, INDIA
MATHAROO ASSOCIATES

5,800 square feet
Builder/Contractor: J K Constructions
Structural Design: Rushabh Consultancy
Interior Design: Matharoo Associates
Landscape Design: Matharoo Associates
pp. 158–67

COURTYARD RESIDENCE, 2020
SEATTLE, WA, USA
MWWORKS

3,480 square feet
Builder/Contractor: Dowbuilt Structural
Engineers: PCS Structural Solutions, J Welch Engineering
Interior Design: Studio DIAA
Landscape Architect: Wittman Estes
pp. 168–77

CORK HOUSE, 2022
LONDON, UK
POLYSMITHS

1,300 square feet
Builder/Contractor: Enviro Building Company
Engineer: Price & Myers
Interior Design: Polysmiths
Landscape Design: Polysmiths
pp. 178–89

CAN JAIME I N'ISABELLE, 2018
PALMA, MAJORCA, SPAIN
TED'A ARQUITECTES

3,500 square feet
Technical architect: Luis Rivas
Builder: Repack and Joan Sastre
Engineer: Sergi Altariba
pp. 190–201

IGLOO, 2021
MOSSEL BAY, SOUTH AFRICA
YVZA

3,700 square feet
Builder/Contractor: Eric Waterson (Procon)
Engineer: Cobus Louw
Interior Design: YvZa
pp. 202–9

CLIFTON HILL COURTYARD HOUSE, 2022
CLIFTON HILL, AUSTRALIA
STUDIO MKN + ELIZA BLAIR ARCHITECTURE

2,400 square feet
Builder/Contractor: Kleev Homes
Engineer: PD Structures
Interior Design: Studio MKN
Landscape Design: Peachy Green
pp. 210–17

IMAGE CREDITS

Leonardo Shieh 16–29; Tom Ross, Courtesy Breathe Architecture 30–41; Yasunori Shimomura 42–49; © Dove Dope, Courtesy Práctica Arquitectura 50–51; © Apertura Arquitectónica, Courtesy Práctica Arquitectura 54, 58–59, 60, 62; © César Béjar, Courtesy Práctica Arquitectura 52–53, 55, 56, 57, 61 top and bottom, 63; Tom Ferguson 64–73; © Tim Van de Velde 74–75, 76, 81; © Bruno Vanbesien 77, 78, 79; © Darren Bradley 82–91; Jack Hobhouse 92–99; Hanna Michelson 100–109; Ema Peter, Courtesy Leckie Studio 110–19; Rory Gardiner 120–27; © Clinton Weaver 128–29, 131, 132, 133, 135; © Alisha Gore 130; Hiroyuki Oki 136–47; Timothy Hursley 148–57; Photography © Edmund Sumner / @edmundsumner 158–59, 164–65; Courtesy Matharoo Associates 160, 162; Bharath Ramamrutham 161, 163, 166–67; © Kevin Scott 168–77; Photo Lorenzo Zandri 178–79, 180, 188–89; Photo French & Tye, The Modern House 181–87; TEd'A Arquitectes 190–91, 194, 195, 196, 199 top and bottom; Luis Díaz Díaz 192–93, 197, 198, 200–201; Photo Warren Heath, Bureaux 202–207; Frances Marais, Courtesy YvZA 209; © Shannon McGrath 210–217.

ACKNOWLEDGMENTS

A PERSONAL NOTE

As a bookish writer, home has always been very important to me. It's a quiet place to retreat to, just as nature is for me. So, it has been such a treasure to work on this book, in which the two come together so thoughtfully.

Thank you to my parents for allowing me to grow up in homes that embodied the two, and for your lifelong support of all I do.

To my mother, thank you for your shared appreciation of architecture. It's your vision that made my childhood homes so cozy and comfortable. Thank you for all our drives looking at houses.

To my father, my fellow reader, I am truly my father's daughter and proud of it.

To my sister, one of my biggest cheerleaders, and a lifelong best friend.

To my dear friend Suchi, thank you for your positivity, constant support, and our ongoing thread. You are truly a light in my life.

To my in-laws, who have always invited me into their beautiful world with open arms and all cotton.

And to Roman, my own private architect. Thank you for looking at plans for me and helping me to see what I can't see. Thank you for giving me the time, space, and quiet to write. And so much more.

COLLABORATION

To the architects whose projects are included in this book: Thank you for answering my long list of questions and then some. Thank you for your artful, respectful incorporation of nature, air, and light into these exceptional homes. We need more of that. And thanks to your teams in their entirety. It takes a village, not one person, to design and build a home. And to those whose projects did not make it into the book, it was certainly not for lack of vision, but logistics. I thank you for your time.

To the landscape architects, your ability to simultaneously draw attention to and weave the greenery through and into these homes with a whisper stirs a sense of awe.

Thank you to the homeowners who have allowed this intimate look into your private worlds.

Thank you to the photographers, whose vision is the heart of this book. Full stop.

To Melanie Mues, the incredible book designer. Your unexpected and surprising choices just feel so right. Thank you for making me more than proud to call this book my own and yours.

And of course, thank you to the team at Monacelli and Phaidon. First and foremost, to my editor, Jenny Florence. Thank you for so closely including me in the process from start to finish, it means the world to me. Thank you for your shared vision. To Alan Rapp, who helped me through the contract process and answered my myriad questions when Jenny was on maternity leave at the start of this project. To production director Michael Vagnetti, thank you for guiding the ship. And to Deborah Aaronson, who kicked it all off by sharing my initial proposal email with Jenny. And to all the other members of the Monacelli crew (shout out to Caroline Jones on the marketing and publicity team) who have made this book what it is and put it out into the world with such care.

A CONNECTION TO NATURE

Through all these years writing about architecture, I have always found myself seeking out nature in the homes and other spaces and places I've stepped into. As I enter a room, my eye is naturally drawn to the window and the green world outside of it. This strong connection to nature, which is what all these courtyard homes share, is ultimately what drew me to the idea of this book. Growing up in a house on a hill surrounded by forest instilled this deep connection. As a result, my ideal world is one where there is nature inside and out. This book feels like a little piece of that. So, to nature, thank you for being a guiding light in my life, always and forever. May you get the reverence you deserve.

MONACELLI
A Phaidon Company
111 Broadway
New York, NY 10006

Phaidon Press Limited
2 Cooperage Yard
London E15 2QR

Phaidon SARL
55, rue Traversière
75012 Paris

phaidon.com/monacelli

First published 2025

ISBN 978-1-58093-705-4

Library of Congress Control Number:
2025939488

Editor: Jenny Florence
Production: Michael Vagnetti
Design: Melanie Mues,
Mues Design, London

Printed in China